# To Light The Trails

Poems About Women In A Violent World

## An Anthology

Edited by Annick Yerem, Sue Finch, Mo Schoenfeld,
Sarah Connor, Giovanna MacKenna
and Róisín Ní Neachtain.

# To Light The Trails
Poems About Women In A Violent World
An Anthology

Edited by Annick Yerem, Sue Finch, Mo Schoenfeld,
Sarah Connor, Giovanna MacKenna
and Róisín Ní Neachtain.

Legal Notice. Annick Yerem, Sue Finch, Mo Schoenfeld, Sarah Connor, Giovanna MacKenna and Róisín Ní Neachtain have asserted their rights under section 77 of the Copyright, Designs & Patents Act 1988 to be identified as the editors of this work. Individual contributors reserve copyright to their work. Cover art work by Annick Yerem (age 8) and Katherine Inglis-Meyer, All Rights Reserved. No part of this book may be reproduced, stored in a retrieval system, or transmitted in any form, or by any means; electronic, mechanical, photopcopying, without prior permission from the editors/authors. However short extracts may be quoted on social media.

Published 2024 by Sidhe Press
https://sidhe-press.eu

Design and dedication illustration by Jane Cornwell
www.janecornwell.co.uk

Also from Sídhe Press:

Our Own Coordinates
Poems About Dementia - An Anthology

The Crow Gods
Sarah Connor

Glisk and Glimmer
Poems About Light - An Anthology

Just One More Before I Go
Nikki Dudley

Dedication

Annick:
For Hind Rajab. For Dr. Ameera Elasouli.

Sarah:
To my daughter, and all her beautiful friends, young women navigating a difficult world.

Sue:
For all the women who have shown me how to walk in the world. I am a better person because of you.

Trigger Warning

When we walk as women in a violent world, we face multiple challenges. Those expressed in the following pages include: the threat of physical, sexual and domestic violence; abuse; suicide ideation; self-harm; racial profiling and murder.

# Introduction

First of all, we want to thank all our contributors. You put your trust in us and we know how much it takes to do that, especially with poems as brave and vulnerable as those now held in these pages. We are in awe of you all.

This is an important anthology for us. We have all known or experienced some sort of violence. Women are not safe in this world, be it at home, on the streets, with the people close to them or due to the actions of their own or foreign governments. We cannot name them all, but we acknowledge all the victims of femicide, the women who are fighting to be heard and respected, and the women who are victims of genocide, currently in Gaza, and recently in Ethiopia and Myanmar, and throughout history, as well as those women in places like Afghanistan and Iran, who have also been forsaken by the inaction of our governments to intervene to protect them.

It is not naïve to hope for a better world, it is not naïve to fight for it.

The Sídhe Team

# Contents

| | | |
|---|---|---|
| 8 | Beth Brooke | *Childhood Ambition* |
| 10 | Ronita Chattopadhyay | *Shall I Tell You About My First Heartbreak?* |
| 12 | Roxane Llanque | *Black Pocket Knife* |
| 14 | Larissa Reid | *Haunted* |
| 15 | Giovanna MacKenna | *How to find your face in the dark – 1987* |
| 16 | Christina Daub | *My Mother Teaches me the Uselessness of No* |
| 18 | Jane Killingbeck | *The Survivor* |
| 20 | Emma Galloway Stephens | *My Grandmother's Ghost and I Watch Our Home Burn* |
| 22 | Lucy Heuschen | *Wimbledon Common* |
| 24 | Sarah-Jane Crowson | *Spelling Test* |
| 25 | Allison Black | *Mid-Forties Family Man* |
| 26 | Abigail Ottley | *Exposure* |
| 28 | Jane Carroll | *Advice to my daughter* |
| 30 | Kerry Darbishire | *Hunted* |
| 32 | Róisín Ní Neachtain | *Was I Born To Lie Still?* |
| 34 | Nicola Heaney | *Crowning Glory* |
| 36 | Margaret Royall | *Wolf Moon Haunts After A Night At The Palais* |
| 38 | Ger Duffy | *Somewhere in Ulcinq* |
| 40 | Julia Biggs | *Bystreet* |
| 41 | Annick Yerem | *Untitled* |
| 42 | Sue Finch | *Palm Your Keys and Keep Your Thumb Out* |
| 43 | Lynne Jensen Lampe | *(don't) take me home* |
| 44 | Lucy Heuschen | *Asclepius, God of Surgery* |
| 46 | Louise Machen | *The Bus Station is Closed for Resurfacing* |
| 47 | Shasta Hanif Ali | *Meri Zaban* |

| | | |
|---|---|---|
| 50 | Annick Yerem | *There is only one dark alleyway in this poem* |
| 52 | Mo Schoenfeld | *GBVerses* (Tanka Triptych) |
| 54 | Tamiko Dooley | *Nomikai (After-work drinks)* |
| 56 | Angela France | *Elegies for The Women* |
| 58 | Kitty Donnelly | *Much To Lose* |
| 59 | Margaret Poynor-Clark | *Brain Surgery* |
| 60 | Moira J. Saucer | *Winter, 1978* |
| 62 | Yvonne Reddick | *Kinder Stones* |
| 64 | Sarah Stockton | *Real* |
| 65 | Sarah Connor | *Iphigenia's nails* |
| 66 | Sharon SingingMoon | *Decreasing Pressure* |
| 68 | Lynne Jensen Lampe | *Bob Dylan Warned Them* |
| 70 | Ger Duffy | *Me Too Bingo* |
| 72 | Chaucer Cameron | *Dredging Up the River* |
| 73 | Giovanna MacKenna | *Key/hole* |
| 74 | Attracty Fahy | *The White Chair* |
| 76 | Jane Burn | *Gob Quiet* |
| 78 | Merril D. Smith | *This is How The Story Ends* |
| 79 | Afsaneh Gitiforouz | *Daughters of The Sun* |
| 82 | Yvonne Reddick | *Moon, I call you as Witness* |
| 84 | Anna Shelton | *The Metaphor* |
| 86 | Kitty Donnelly | *Deposition Site* |
| 88 | Oormila Vijayakrishnan Prahlad | *Doll's Eyes* |
| 90 | Anon | *The Saddest Place* |
| 91 | Beth Brooke | *Naqba* |
| 92 | Anna Shelton | *The One Time I Call 999 The Police Are Having A Party* |
| 93 | Sarah Connor | *Untitled* |
| 94 | Sharon SingingMoon | *Kemonomichi* |
| 95 | Alice Stainer | *Street Talking* |
| 96 | - | Biographies |
| 101 | - | Acknowledgements |

# Childhood Ambition
Beth Brooke

This child is small
      round-faced   just out of infancy
and fiercely alive
      I watch her climb ladders
launch herself down slides
      traverse those rope-net bridges
intended for much older children

see her haul herself
      hand over hand
to the further side
she knows she is
      without limits

even when I power the swing
   she commands
knows what she wants   higher
faster
      higher  faster  more  more

she chooses
this child who gleams like opal

       is all rainbow colours that
crackle and spark
she is a kite that dances
on the wind

I watch as she learns the world
learns the edges of herself
       grows powerful
and I am afraid

I am afraid for the day when
someone tells her     no
she does not command
her own being no
her body   is not  her own
tells her    no
kite flying is forbidden
      tells her to close her mouth
to cover her strong arms
her legs   her face   her everything
tells her she is
a provocation tells her    no

# Shall I Tell You About My First Heartbreak?

Ronita Chattopadhyay

I must have been 12 years old

and I was learning kathak.

You know the warmth, the giddiness of love?

I felt all that in the magical beats of the tabla,

the rapturous response of ghungroos.

I was lost in the alchemy of the sounds

and stories my body could tell.

The giddiness could have been

from the chakkars though.

And then it was over.

Because Masterji kept changing the timings.


4pm to 5pm became 5pm to 6pm, then 6.30 to 7.30

and that was my undoing.

*It gets dark. It is not safe for a girl outside then.*

*Your dance classes will have to stop.*

The ghungroos were moved from my table
to the top most drawer in the cupboard
above my reach.
I would not need them again.
I walked around in a daze for weeks
hugging close that cloak of hurt and heavy sadness.

I still can't hold ghungroos in my hand.
But I do dance when I am happy, or sad.

Kathak: a classical, north Indian dance form.
Tabla: a pair of small hand drums.
Chakkars: a circle, or spin dance movement.
Ghungroos: small metallic bells (strung together on ropes or sewed on cotton/velvet cloth) tied to the dancer's ankles.

# Black Pocket Knife

Roxane Llanque

I was six when I learned the threat of rape
from a news report I wasn't supposed to hear

I need not fear all men
my father assured me
as he carried with him
a veiled knife of Switzerland
a country of neutral reliability.

I wondered
how anyone can be neutral
when this is what a girl learns
she has to fear
when she is six years old?

I learned mourning then
the girl I was an hour before
the girl who did not know
she had to carry a concealed defense
as not to offend the offenders.

I learned black

was the color of mourning

so by morning

I asked my father

very neutrally

for a black pocket knife

to feel safe from that threat

those four shadowed letters

this neutral world

would place

on a six-year-old girl.

# Haunted

Larissa Reid

I didn't want you here;

you came nonetheless,

with your wide eyes

and bone feather wings.

You snap your face around

as you quarter my presence,

make as if to touch my cheek

or stroke my neck like you used to.

I recoil from that shivering memory,

so you tilt away

and skirt the walled rim of the field;

a deliberate taunting.

My heart splits along seams

spilling red, like autumn's last poppies along the verge.

# How to find your face in the dark – 1987

Giovanna MacKenna

A long time ago, when this body was smaller, finer, still growing, I climbed from my borrowed bedroom window out onto midnight grass. I had waited until the house was still, the voices softened to snores and sobs, the cat fur-rich in the crook of my arm, the waves were at their loudest. The plunge from house to out had shucked my childhood shell, left me bold and glisteningly unburdened. Each footfall soothed stifled emotions, caressed my numbness. Finally, gasping, I found the water. Its liquorice waves were calling an old friend's welcome; the sea's voice filled the silence as it listened to the ache of unsaid words.

Later, after a tearful farewell, as I swam my way into the depths of those vacant streets, my steps were no longer alone. I felt a man at my back, carefully gaining ground, his feet matched the rev of my breath, the upward tic of my heart. As long-taught panic threatened, I thought of my parent the water; of how it knows when to whisper, of the fearsome strength of its ire. I let him almost reach me before turning to unleash a bellow, rich with all my smothered rage, straight into his sweated face. He ran. I stood, triumphant, breathless with power, gulping air now pungent with the tang of my own voice. Once the echoes died, I tucked my sound back inside, kept the miracle safe, before climbing back through the window into that still dark house.

# My Mother Teaches me the Uselessness of No
Christina Daub

Don't make eye contact. Always look
like you know where you're going,
even if you don't. Walk fast. Rotate
the eye in the back of your head to stay
vigilant at all times. Never acknowledge
catcalls, strangers, random comments.
Vary your route and make sure no one
is following you. If you think someone
is following you, go into a public place
and call a friend to pick you up
and escort you home. You can't trust
security guards. Policemen aren't
what they used to be. Don't think
because a man looks like a grandpa,
he can't overpower you. If you have
to go out, wear men's clothing:
a loose shirt, baggy pants, shoes
you can run in. Keep your glasses on.
Gain some weight. You might be tall,
but girls like you can be snapped
in two. Men only want one thing.
Remember that. Don't let him

buy you a drink and whatever
you order for yourself, never take
your eyes off it. Carry it with you
into the ladies room. Don't let him
touch your arm, your back, your hair.
That just encourages him. Whatever
you do, don't let him kiss you. It's all
over then. Do you mean to tell me
after everything I've taught you,
a man still broke you open like an egg?
What did you do, smile?
Didn't I tell you, to never, ever smile?

# The Survivor
Jane Killingbeck

The night bus sways, lurches,
edges into a kerbside, here its final passenger –

the last streetlight until home.
through vantablack, shadowless,

a dark copse holds no fear. You grow
with the wood, understand its wild listening,

limbs of trees I once climbed stretch
above wenge branches, dens

dug by creatures and you a childhood
ago. Night holds excitement in the sky,

home ever closer calls your name,
love in the kitchen lingering.

Sudden sounds, skew, crack the silence
small life scuttles, not a fox

panting, but malice moving in,
a sudden movement lunges swipes

blocks your place on the moonless path,
a slab of shadow steps into your space.

You swerve, twist, zig zag, it runs, but you run faster
breathlessness falls in through the door of home,

gasps of understanding disbelief
a father springs up, capture in his feet,

his chase now, you grasp a mother's hand,
lights brighten the trees of your childhood wood,

police dogs search sniff and poke in under-scrub.
You fear the end of someone.

# My Grandmother's Ghost and I Watch Our Home Burn

Emma Galloway Stephens

I stood elbow deep in smoke

curling from the rubble of my old house

knowing now that I could not step

through doors that would never open again

Beginnings sometimes open at the end

of old stories   The monster that made

ghosts out of my grandmothers

no longer walks the woods, no longer

breathes fire from the furnace I fear

This is my story

no one else can tell

The spell broke when I drove

a burning stake into the wheel

looking at my granddaughter

I see a new heaven and a new earth

over this land I used to call a paradise

Grandchildren are authors of peace

I am a specter that haunts the pages

my bleeding mouth a memory

legacy   There's no more tomorrow for me   She

weaves stories from pine needles and smoke

I am old    I no longer believe

my home is gone forever

that my heritage has no chance to sing

my heart into the echo

of time

# Wimbledon Common

Lucy Heuschen

Here I stood with graph paper,
clipboard, sharpened HB pencil
and you, certain as a geography project.
Here is the pond we paced,
scavenging data for our report
until our footsteps became the path.
Here is the place that claimed a careless child.
Here is the flat plain of Caesar's Camp,
the gravel trap where your bike slid out
and we peeled back tatty cords
to discover a pale poke of shin-bone.
Here is the hollow heart of the laurels
where we chased a long ball
and found a rubbing, grinning man.
Here are the badger tracks we stumbled on,
slurping stolen cider. Here is sunburnt grass,
plastic-bag-blankets, kicked-off sandals,
stubs of Silk Cut. Here is the spot you ran from
when we fought. Here is a black mirror
shrouded with firs, a shadow
stalking the treeline. Maybe here
is the place that claimed a careless child.

Here is the Bouncing Tree, its screech

of sugared children like green parakeets.

Here are two hazy girls, striding past

like we've somewhere else to be.

Like this place isn't carved into us,

pocket-knifed, dread magic, sigil scar.

# Spelling Test

Sarah-Jane Crowson

It always started with a tiny slip.
A hot day. I'd maybe moved your tea,
opened the door. That was enough to trip
you into throwing books. You hated me

and all my arts. And so my words were hung,
strung up at night like dead things pinned on lines.
Outside the wailing dark fluttered and sung -
and beat its wings and turned to moths (divine

and dusty compasses). They lit the trails
of fragile wildness - led me back through time
towards the gods of leaves and light and snails–
the curled fern, the tangled mess of vine.

It's broken now, your spell, and though my words
have not quite yet grown wings, they breathe, are heard.

# Mid-Forties Family Man

Allison Black

the whole time

while his hands are on me

and later, fleeing, jostled on the tram

when they aren't but I can still feel them

and at home in the shower

scalding water and soap and scrubbing

and still I can feel him on me

I am telling myself

my thoughts looping and loud

that I am only seventeen

and no one will believe me

and he is my boss

and I need the job to pay my rent

and no one else is going to save me

and I was only cashing up my till

but maybe it's my fault anyway, right?

*stay still*

the whole time

*keep quiet*

# Exposure *(somewhere near Kendal, the mid-1960's)*
Abigail Ottley

Mud-lagged and shoeless, I am cold, afraid.
Three-quarters blind, half asleep.

I cannot run. You have thrown away
my glasses. Rain blinds me, too

Your long legs carry you further, faster so
you drag me like a carcass in your wake

In your head you are both hunter and hunted,
Geronimo, heading for the hills.

A man full-grown, but I see through you. One of
us is not a proper grown-up

Here is a window, lit yellow in the gloom.
Rain-sleet slices me raw.

I think I might die here,
never go home.

*Please stop now,*
I sob into the wind.

Hours have passed since the blade
of your hunting knife

hacked at my hair.

# Advice to my daughter
Jane Carroll

Not that road. Not that one either. Pick
the ones with good light with busy
shops and bystanders and houses where the
windows are lit and the curtains left open.
Wear shoes like these ones. That's right. And hold
your keys just so, between your knuckles, like claws.
Yes. I know. I know.
Just call if you want a lift. It doesn't matter what time.
It's not like I'll sleep until I know you're home.
And tell a friend if you're getting a cab. Two friends.
Yes, I know. I know.
And you have to walk calmly. With purpose. Head up.
Don't run. Well, not unless you have to.
Learn to scream. Not for help. Never for help.
My mother told me that nobody would come to help.
She told me to shout "fire!"
I know. Yes, I know.
Me? Not counting the ones who did nothing really.
The ones who just followed for a bit.
The ones who called out but then left me alone.
The other kind? The bad kind?
I've been lucky. Only a couple of times.

A handful. A few. Enough. Enough
that I've learned all these things that I know.
I know. I know. I know.

# Hunted

Kerry Darbishire

I became bruin bear

to mask the way I looked –

hungry through Autumn bracken

walking fearless as a foggy night.

My steps into the unknown did not falter

each one was a serious moon.

In the darkest corners

I sung the song of her

to all the night flowers so bright

we belonged to each other.

Through distance and more distance

I breathed the fire of my mother

fells of my father rising to the stars

and when a shadow swayed the ground

and water reached my throat

I thought of my children not yet born

held my phone like the brawn

of a hogglestack and loaded messages

of winter fuel into my bones. Each crack

and split behind me through the tree-heavy lane

was the path I knew and trusted. I would not

turn around or show my tears and swore no one

would hear my heart beating like feral paws

or find me young – a fallen tree in wet turf.

The brown bear is sometimes referred to as the *bruin*, from Middle English.

Hogglestack: Cumbrian dialect for wooden chopping block.

# Was I Born To Lie Still?
Róisín Ní Neachtain

I unwrap my skin

every night after my bath.

How now rose-cast breast,

wretch of nipple,

time-faced and unmade.

How I learn to pick off the scars

of my skin,

fashioned from anger,

clay-shaped from rib

of failed man.

Obsolete

and obese,

backward figure,

anticlimax colour

held at heel by men.

Was there a summer's game

where heavy moon-crested fists

turned to a flutter

innocent as a stream

as if dawn was heaven?


Was I born to lie still

with *my my my* still mouth?


I palm the disobedience

of my wounds,

push my legs forward-motion

to different tides of history.

# Crowning Glory
Nicola Heaney

There she is, our Rapunzel,
tucked under the eaves
sitting cross-legged on the floor
of her little attic room.

Watch as chestnut strands
land on shoulders, legs, feet –
still-born snakes severed
in the buzz of blunt clippers.

She rubs her hands
over a film of fuzz
thumbs probing the nape
she explores her skull

the ridge on her crown
from the topple down stairs
which fractured her skull

that indent on her left temple
from when she was knocked
into the sideboard

those little bald patches
from the cigarette burns
hidden behind her ears.

Catching her reflection
on the window,
eyes moons in a tiny head,

she throws up the sash,
turns her too-big face
to the night
and howls.

# Wolf Moon Haunts After A Night At The Palais

Margaret Royall

As muffled clocks strike midnight black
an unknown monster prowls the city streets.

Clouds in the blotting paper sky
seep pools of darkest fantasy.

She walks a concrete wilderness;
villas with hollow eyes glare down,
turrets zoom from gothic pasts.

On Gallows Hill a scaffold shape
looms through the rough-sewn cloak of night…

Last bus gone, taxis on strike.

She scurries home, a galleon in full sail,
her Jimmy Choos click-clacking
on the slippery cobblestones.

*Beware the bad moon rising!*
that's what the locals said…

*Just stupid talk* she tells herself,

yet pleads for fair winds, following seas,

hoping for a tidal wave to carry her safely home.

She startles at every sudden sound:

fighting toms on cracked tin roofs,

drink cans whistling past her feet.

But... just in case, she grasp her keys and phone,

thumb hovering over 9.

# Somewhere in Ulcinq

Ger Duffy

All day, black clad women shook their heads
when we asked for *soba* or *zimmer*. We trudged
the curve of that scooped out bay to every
whitewashed house as the landscape wavered.

Men watched us behind hooded lids, young girls
fingered our hair and clothes until dusk swallowed
the last light. Violins sang with the waves, colored
lights danced by the shore, glasses clattered in bars,

our skin reeked of fried fish and garlic. I sat
on a low wall as the full face of a yellow moon rose.
Upside down fishing boats proved unsuitable for sleeping.
We reached the end of the beach accompanied by

stray cats, lapping waves. Dark trees, sharp against
the night sky followed us uphill until we arrived
at a clearing. Pia sat down, I stood – looked ahead,
then to each side, then behind where I saw two

white teeshirts, crouched low, staring back. Pia asked,
*What is? RUN*, I said *RUN*, we threw ourselves

at darkness, trees crashed and fell, the ground rose
to cut our arms and legs, the sky fell, righted itself,

fell again; we slipped down that hill like two Jills.
What might happen to two Jills, happened to us.
Later, we arrived at the *Milica* where they viewed
us under peaked caps and muttered *"Bre, bre."*

Something about our dirty shorts and torn tops
angered them. We used their toilet with its stack
of porn mags, greasy lights and beauty calendar.
We slept sitting upright outside, until goat bells

woke us. Retracing our steps, we found our passports,
tickets and scattered underwear, we seized each item
as if they might speak back to us. As the ancient bus
arrived, we embraced its arthritic doors, as if it was

our mothers' womb, come to take us home. As that bus
creaked along the steep coast road, I thought
of my mother, of how we would go on being pursued,
our daughters,              their daughters.

# Bystreet

Julia Biggs

A shortcut,

a shortcut found,

a shortcut found cutoff.

A shortcut like the full stop

found in his stopper-tight sneer.

A shortcut curdled like your fear-taut blood,

curdled and clotted with his already-sour catcall tongue.

# Untitled

Annick Yerem

                women    freedom    peaceful assembly

                                    women        can
advocate                                                  for
women

          women's voices are           meaningfully
included

                                                      women's
rights              in conflict
                                       women and
                    girls, are
                                               the real
litmus test

                  we are failing this test.
safety of women

affected by conflict,                crucial
       in conflict resolution, peacebuilding,
                                    women

              continue      strongly
              in      peace

# Palm Your Keys and Keep Your Thumb Out

Sue Finch

You buy me a long key that unlocks nothing
tell me to palm it when walking home alone.
You say keep some white on your nails –
if they come close a scratch will hold DNA.

I say I don't carry much cash
I can just hand it over
show them there is no need
to bother with me.

Your eyes tell me
it is not about the money
and I plan my hammer grip.

# (don't) take me home

Lynne Jensen Lampe

*golden shovel after*

*concrete blonde's* take me home

i cry-count names :: bars :: tongues :: so
      what if i don't
believe any of you ::
      what if i hear desire cry
*pretty clit* but close every throat :: it'll
      strip my shame :: i'll forgive
myself for each of you
      :: for every memory :: crossed lines
respect wet sand :: you toss truth around
      like flies :: what i mean is i unwant your
bodies :: what i mean is unhunger your eyes

# Asclepius, God of Surgery

Lucy Heuschen

*- This poem is dedicated to the women of the NHS.*

What if he isn't kind. If his staff
shields him. If we have no option
but snake-worship. What if we've
done our homework like he said,
only to find it changes nothing.

What if we must gown him daily,
arms outspread in the scrub room
like Christ the Redeemer over Rio.
What if oblivion lurks just outside
the bright perimeter of his hands.

What if he schedules us for nights,
bending us double over the altar
of our vocation. What if —NO—
is not in his lexicon. If we're told
to grow up, calm the fuck down.

What if the truth slips, green-scaled

from under his mask:

a small man / a fist / a knife.

Note: Asclepius is the Greco-Roman god of medicine and surgery. He is typically pictured as a bearded, kindly man, holding a staff with a serpent wrapped around it, which is still the symbol of the medical profession today.

# The Bus Station is Closed for Resurfacing
Louise Machen

           I will have to get off the stop before,
beside the woods, across from the garage
where you order from the window at this time of night.
Trees eat the dimly lit shelter and a dirt track filters out
onto the pavement, past an old wall on the threshold
of traffic and the dark beyond its greenery.

Taking out my left earphone,
                  I tread the tightrope
of kerb and passing cars and things that might exist beyond
the gap in the brick: this ginnel of night-time imaginings.
I clench my fist, right elbow firmly fixed on shoulder bag,
swift look ahead and to the left, careful not to trip into the road,
step quickening, thinking of home,
              praying that I live to see
                          the bus station when it's finished.

# Meri Zaban

Shasta Hanif Ali

I think of languages - how they travel over continents

crossing thresholds, one foot in one country

a heel in another. When the towers fell

our zaban hid in the folds of our hijabs.

On every commute, fear filled the empty seats beside us


Insha—

Bismill—

Alhumdu—


Unfinished sentences hang in an air thick with suspicion

of people     like us


Some languages are

stopped     and

searched     and

lined up more often than others


We arrive at the airport 4 hours early — that's 2 hours

earlier than you

     because *random* is a uniform interrogating

Why are you visiting?      Where will you be staying?

And he frisks you            and he pats you
and he holds you             pending further investigation
In a long winding row of passengers, sniffer dogs fetch
a brightly coloured ball landing
at no other feet      but ours

The gap widens between them      and us
as the dogs come to sniff once again     *just to be sure.*

At *random,* our baby bag is emptied — twice,
all milk bottles  &  nappies  &  sudocreme

Our children's hands are *randomly* swept.
Not once.     Not twice.     But thrice.

*Baby, It's just a game,  you'll play forever.*
     we reassure gazelle eyes

scanning         scanning         scanning         our faces.

Your shoes, and His shoes,

are removed to a light chorus of relief

from others          othering you


Only when our family is cleared through security,

       crayons spilling a rainbow across polished floors

do strangers eyes meet yours again,

crinkling nervously at corners


And it's here,

I see how customs of land & place

can make us

       & break us.


Meri zaban: my language

# There is only one dark alleyway in this poem
Annick Yerem

The police never knew

About the boy who held my head down
outside the disco
About the boy I broke up with who said
*I could kill you*
About the man who left me nowhere to escape to
About the boy who hadn't told me
his parents weren't home
About the man who shouted, *if you don't get out of
the car now, I will beat you to death*
About the man who stuck his tongue down my
throat because he felt I was *easy*

There is only one dark alleyway in this poem
There are homes and places and daylight

I didn't say no
I didn't run
I held my breath and held
my body

I thought I deserved this.

This disregard for my life, my

fearlessness, my

sinews, my

smile, my way out.

# GBVerses (Tanka Triptych)
Mo Schoenfeld

## *Old BMV*

Soothing, evening stroll,

tunes and sunset, solitude,

all the weight, lifting.

wheels, slick with stealth, and silent,

'are you okay alone, love?'

## *Single track road*

"I'm good. We live here."

(None of your bloody business!)

'Ah, privileged lady.

You should wear a pullover,

it's getting colder outside.'

## Made for walking

Mumble of "good night",

hiking boots pick up the pace,

of their own accord.

Breath-sharp petrichor, ploughed field,

low crunch of tyres grows faint.

# Nomikai (After-work drinks)

Tamiko Dooley

I don't remember

When the *yuzu* sake was being poured

I don't remember

Why we stood alone outside

I don't remember

How we ended up in the taxi

I don't remember

Your *genkan*

But I remember

Half-falling asleep

I remember

Needing help climbing the stairs

I remember

Your sweat-soaked face
Grinning in half-*kurasa*

And I.

Remember.

Saying.

No.

# Elegies for The Women

Angela France

Somebody asked what she was wearing
Sarah was just walking home from a friend
You should take care to stay in well-lit areas
Naomi was stabbed in her flat

Sarah was just walking home from a friend
her family miss her all the time
Naomi was stabbed in her flat
her neighbours say they heard screaming

Her family miss her all the time
Kathleen fell from a third floor window
her neighbours say they heard screaming
Lauren was run over twice by her father

Kathleen fell from a third floor window
Her ex-boyfriend was charged with murder
Lauren was run over twice by her father
He was in a rage and wanted to kill her

Her ex-boyfriend was charged with murder
Ailish was pregnant with her fifth child
He was in a rage and wanted to kill her
she was a beautiful, amazing young woman

Ailish was pregnant with her fifth child
Brianna was only 16, found in a park
she was a beautiful, amazing young woman
Hina was found in a suitcase, in a ditch

Brianna was only 16, found in a park
You should take care to stay in well-lit areas
Hina was found in a suitcase, in a ditch
Somebody asked what she was wearing

# Much To Lose
Kitty Donnelly

As I blossom into the mother I coveted,
the head drops from its stalk,
a rose beheaded. We share
an umbrella on Broad Street,
discussing your intrusive thoughts
as mutant strains of history
revise our futures. In Wendy News,
papers imply the struck
have the temerity to die
amongst the rubble of their enemy.

You say you choose *the victim's
shoes, the underdog, the litter's runt,*
mining for metaphors, bent
on a eutopia that's out of reach,
unshakable womb-dreams.
In University Parks, a flare of leaves
cat-sneak through outstretched palms
a magpie performs its balancing
dance on a bench and we're wild
for superstitions: antidotes to chaos.

# Brain Surgery

Margaret Poynor-Clark

He says all my complaints are inside my head
as I watch him rotate his index finger
doing his "She is loco" routine,
screwing his screwdriver
metaphorically into my brain.

It starts bit by bit,
drilling out the white matter
going deeper into the grey.
I watch my cerebral porridge trickle
onto his operating theatre floor,
creating an air of indecision, fuzzy thinking,
losing a bit more every day,
I'm starting to doubt myself,
deciding I must be, "Going loco" after all.

# Winter, 1978

Moira J. Saucer

From New Mexico, we hitch south.
Blood burns under cold Texas stars.

You spent my money on seed beads.
Dark money for blood won't feed her.

Louisiana, Alabama.
Then--two tickets home--Virginia.

Piercing the amniotic sea,
our bond-in-blood destroyed.

It will be a savage winter,
a rented room for this scourged womb.

Let me shake off the scent, and lose
the bloodhound of marriage, family.

The sidewalks swell with heavy snow,
the Delaware cold pulses this heart.

God, please forgive me if

I am not enough am not sufficient.

# Kinder Stones
Yvonne Reddick

In my mind's eye, a rock transforms
to a roebuck's head, then as I pass
it flattens to a flounder, swimming in rain.

Further along, an Iguanodon eye
scratched into another boulder, pebbles for teeth.

> Kindly stones, hide me. Even here, I hear
> his tread on the stair.

The Woolpacks: petrified sheep
and Ice Age beasts that plummeted off the edge
of the last long thaw.

> Wherever I go, will he lie in wait.
> Madwoman's Stones, Chapelgate.

Druid Stone, wind-sculpture, altar of rain.
Sour peat beneath the wind's muttering.
A burnt-out summer, bog beacon
sprouting alight on moor-pools.

> The cowering hare of my fear.

      Leave no trace. Cover my tracks. No photos.

That distant spring, when the bilberry flowers
were rose lanterns, and his hand in mine was gentle.

Late summer, the whinberry ripened,
their seeds and sharp sweetness
purpling his lifelines.

      It was winter when it started.
      *Shut up. You're crazy. Didn't happen.*

No matter what bearing I take, I return
to these stone herds and moor-lurkers,
the wind ringing through Crowden Tower.

      *Tell no-one, or I'll say you're mad.*
      *Walk behind me. Say nothing.*

I reach the bee-skep of rock, pierced by wind,
smell heath-flowers and willowherb.
My fingers trace the slender blade of my pocket knife.

# Real

Sarah Stockton

What did you do?
I used the wrong cleaner on the bathtub grout.
Didn't pay the phone bill. Paid the phone bill,
should have paid the gas bill instead. *Fucking loser*
Didn't duck. Didn't fuck, fucked too much.
Didn't make enough money. Didn't hand it over.
The meat was undercooked. Overcooked. Too much
fat in the meat, on me, not enough milk in my breasts,
in the tea, *stupid cow*, the bread wasn't fresh, out of
whiskey, what would the relatives think, made me look
like a *white trash bitch*, a *crap cook*, that was all on me.
The children were too loud, the place was a pit, I put
four quarters in the meter when it only needed two.
I was wasteful and an embarrassment, dressed like a
*thrift store slut* when we went out to eat. I wasn't polite
to the waitress, so I had to walk home in the dark. Then
I was late. *Pathetic*. I should have had more self-respect,
not been so weak. I deserved the wrist brace, the bruises,
the tears. *Useless loser* all I did was *bullshit*. Not a real
woman. Not a real mother. Not a real poet.

# Iphigenia's nails

Sarah Connor

Ten pale moons – buffed and shimmering.

Ten pink shells, gathered on a windless shore.

Ten crusted crescents, blackened, torn.

Keep your nails long enough to scratch.

The scratching proves you fought.

# Decreasing Pressure:

*practicing the art of kintsugi*

Sharon SingingMoon

When the weather is damp, an ache
brings my left wrist into focus
& how I lied
told of a bike wreck to hide his sin
my sin - to stay
another year

Muay Thai fighters
beat their shins against banana trees
the micro-tears heal stronger
a golden repair of sorts -
to learn our weaknesses
where to let the glowing liquid flow
to mend a cracked bone
a heart wound
how to walk among the golden leaves
as they fall

I am now

a glorious tapestry

bound with golden seams

celebrating that which has been broken

& repaired

made stronger

# Bob Dylan Warned Them

Lynne Jensen Lampe

The harmonipocalypse
bangs on the gates of Eden,

never used, no ears to hear.
Cowry shells sing a song

of circles & the sea, the plastic
box can see but not remember,

two glass eyes with knobs & dials.
Love is mechanical, smooth,

the moon smooth, lips lapse,
lips laugh, heresy. Drink its salt.

He tells her she has nice knobs,
dissembles her life. Nothing

to remember & nothing to record.
Spool like film, pool like water,

fly away & sing the post-
natural world, sing

of circles & subterranean seas,
choose pleasing shapes.

The harmonipocalyse is now,
fill the cup, sand to glass to marble.

Marble, mar-ble, mar bella,
beautiful sea. Scoop the blues.

She was thirteen when he said
he'd ball her, not nice & not

threatening. She didn't know
what he meant. He grabbed

his camera. Spool like film, pool
like water, wave the inside red.

# #MeToo BINGO

Ger Duffy

*(after Fatimah Ashagar)*

| | | | | |
|---|---|---|---|---|
| A stranger breaks into your room at night. | You wake up with his hand over your mouth. | You are raped from behind. | At first, you refuse to go to the police. | Your main concern is, who else will know this but nothing else about me? |
| You are not that badly hurt (at first) - just bruises, lesions, cuts. | You do not have an STD! | You are not pregnant! | You live on a friend's sofa, too afraid to sleep in your own bed. | You drink to block out his face- this works, most of the time. |
| You remember being pinned down, a pillow over your head, wondering is this just rape? Or am I going to die? | You identify him from a local Employment Agency, cast of characters. | **Free day! Stay inside. Watch boxsets!** Trigger warning - (avoid real-life drama/ crime). | He is charged. | You shave your hair, wear dark glasses, jot down notes for your victim impact statement. |
| While shopping for milk, sanitary towels and cigarettes, you see him on the other side of the store. | You decide not to go to court. | He pleads guilty. | He is given a sentence – one year suspended. | Or you are at a house party. What you remember doesn't make any sense, because it's a friend. |
| You don't remember all, but you do remember flashes. | He would never do what jolts you awake at night, would he? Sometimes you catch him watching you, when you look back, he looks away first. | You do an STD and a pregnancy test. | If you reveal what you think happened to a friend, s/he will look at you and say "Really? Are you sure?" | Just how sure are you really as s/he examines your face for clues? |

# Dredging Up the River

Chaucer Cameron

I'm not sure which comes first, she says to herself

as she negotiates the fourth supermarket aisle,

the abuser turned therapist, or therapist turned abuser.

I'm not certain which comes first, she thinks to herself

as she reaches for six brown eggs from the top shelf,

the gynaecologist abuser, or abuser gynaecologist.

She pushes passed the check out, leaving her half-filled

shopping basket in the middle of the fifth aisle.

It'll be ok to leave it, she mutters, as she leaves the store.

Making her way across the almost empty carpark –

her phone. its bleep. she stops. automatic pilot

and she's back in F block, lying face down in a bath

the sound of electricity buzzing through her brain.

# Key/hole

Giovanna MacKenna

There is a small brass key with a hollow barrel,
the kind that demands pinched fingers and the odd
straining of muscles hidden in front of your knuckles.
Its head is flat and pungent with the ting of old metal.
The barrel is hollow, female, and must be guided, reluctantly,
first slipping off the thrusting pin, to meet its male counterpart.

If you kneel, hands to the floor to knees popping, vulnerable,
careful to keep the tiny key pinched between aching forefinger
and thumb, if you do that, you can peer into the rough wooden
cave and glimpse the lock's jag glinting in its always dark, fixed
and waiting for the inevitable fumble before the forced slide
completes
the match and all that's left is the turn, if your sore bones can take it,

if they're not now locked themselves, frozen in a fake ok when
nothing is.
It's then you look above and see the damage the crowbar did,
how pointless this key's existence is. This place is always open

# The White Chair
Attracty Fahy

Evening closes in, sun setting west, shadows fall
north east of her house, as she leans into the white chair
she'd bought at the end of what was once her life.

She didn't ask which type of wood, it was its light
which drew her. Worn ochre stains, scraped paint,
chipped edges. This chair, a second spine to her place

at the head of the table, where five spindlebacks
in natural pine was home to her family, one empty,
host to the ghost of a father—fear no one named,

until the night her son raged: as if to smash a chair
could restore his trust, his legs wrapped, ankles gripped
around its broken legs, his fists a mandrel to shafts

of mangled wood, and all she could do was sit
on the cold floor, listen to the howl, cries like wolves
at her door. Inside, her children's lives the black limbs

of a leafless tree, the ground a scattering of cherry petals,

their tears an altar to fractured years, the moon a witch,

a broom of dim light through her kitchen.

# Gob Quiet

Jane Burn

Inspired by *Bog Queen,* by Seamus Heaney

I am waste      dead   and haste-buried      shallow
pitted     turf peeled like bad skin      weighted on
my flesh     body a chill stone      gropey-sick
from his palm's traipsed heat
like sick sun     my nylon pelt proved to be
no shield     greedily stripped     noose
of glass beads      unstrung

I am waste      dead   as culled wood      my
pelvis yields     to the pity of the earth's hoard
I still wore the sash
that bound me beautiful     it slipped from my bones
like a dirty stream     I was crowned with sham
glint     the cheap stones lost
their wink     I knew silt

its pebble taste      its slip-wet nestle against

my soiled tongue     my hair has tried to keep to its

cage of grips     I cannot recall

its colour     copper I think     I was caught

        then   I        was

I wish I could tell my mother

*I'm still*    *here*     be warmed in her arms


I wish that I could be birthed from this strange womb

my head holds all

the hollow songs     my grin stays oddly clean

my skull's smile unlipped    he

    covered     my     mouth

*Gob quiet*     he said    *Gob quiet*

*and kiss me*    *so-called queen*

# This is How The Story Ends
Merril D. Smith

Curled like a comma,

as if the conversation had only been paused,

her mouth open, reflected

in the splintered glass ships docked

in myriad red bays--

and his footprints a trail of ellipses

out the bathroom door.

# Daughters of The Sun

Afsaneh Gitiforouz

Women taking off their scarves, burning them,

wearing their hair loose,

heading to fight

They knew death was approaching, and did not fear.

Women cutting their hair, not their hope, to protest, did not fear.

Women defining honour anew,

not by being killed, curled down,

shielding their heads with

their hands behind closed doors

No! This time holding up their heads,

raising their hands high in the streets

battling the honourless, they did not fear

Women making freedom flags like Kaveh`s

from the waves of their own hair.

they were not ashamed

of being a woman, they wouldn´t hide away.

They did not fear.

Stealth freedom no longer enough,

no more longing for the wind to blow through their hair,

no more being openly humiliated, beaten,

killed for saying they exist.

no longer forced to be muted, as if dead while alive,

These women

revealed their being, loudly, and did not fear.

Women whose skulls Zahhaks smashed,

then said they got scared and had a heart attack,

so others would not resist.

These women

became icons of courage and did not fear.

Rising women, brave women,

زن، زندگی، آزادی

on their lips.

They are our daughters.

Daughters of the Sun

Kaveh the Blacksmith – Kāve Āhangar, is a 5000-year-old figure in Iranian mythology who leads a popular uprising against a ruthless foreign ruler, Zahāk. His story is narrated in the Shahnameh, the national epic of Iran (Persia), by the 10th-century Persian poet Ferdowsi.

The Legend of the Serpent King retells the myth of Prince Zahhak who is told by the devil to murder his father and take the throne. Cursed with snakes that grow out his shoulders, he grows infamous throughout the land for his treachery and oppression.

زن، زندگی، آزادی

Zan, Zendegi, Azadi
Woman, Life, Freedom

# Moon, I call you as Witness

Yvonne Reddick

Testify for me. You see girls floating in lakes,
lying in nettles, entombed in concrete floors.
You hear the midnight knock, the call that ends
with a gunshot. Your mouth gapes at the woman
with the moon-round belly
hanging from a tree by a gaunt road.

You peered through a chink in the curtains
at the orbit of my friend's bruise-stained eye.
There are some things that are better whispered
between women – or to you, moon, alone.
His hand squeezing a shriek shut in her throat.
Moon, his fingermarks printed her neck
for a week, my inner sight for months.

The handfuls of pale pills, a brief 'I wish I could live
free' left on the desk. Then the ward's striplights,
frigid and planetary. Needles, bloods.
Her breasts stripped for the heart-trace.
A hushed plea when I arrived – *'Get me out.'*

Moon, this silence is airless. I'm shouting,

my voice a water-drop striking a parched sea.

Moon, help me speak about what you've seen.

# The Metaphor

Anna Shelton

In a feedback group of only women
the tutor says, 'Couldn't you use a metaphor
instead of the word 'rape'?'
another woman says she liked the poem but
why don't I include the perspective of the man?
'The rapist?' I say,
'The man,' she says, 'I'd like to know what he was thinking,'
'his perspective, to balance out the woman.'


So I guess it doesn't matter what you wore
or how fast you ran
when you realised walking was not fast enough
or how much you'd had to drink
or how dark the empty streets were
or how he jumped out from his hiding place
or how you'll never forget his eyes, the smirk upon his face
because what matters is how the metahpor*ist* felt
how did he plan his metaphorical attack
how did he wait so metaquietly in the metaphorical dark
how did he metaphor you on the cold damp concrete
how did he escape the metaphorical police
how did he know he'd be a good metaphor*ist*

how did he metaphor a dozen women

how did he think you would respond

how did he think

how did he

did he

he

# Deposition Site

Kitty Donnelly

If a woman falls in a forest
and no ear hears her
and no eye sees her?
Yes, she falls.

And the trees are cloaks
concealing her killer;
the sphagnum's not
her pillow of choice

for these fragments
of calcium, two boots
and a rag of sleeve.
Listen to them

breathe, the trees,
these instruments of wind,
not telling but singing
a ballad of souls

in foreign terrain,

the song of the severed

lifeline bleeding

from an upturned palm.

# Doll's Eyes

Oormila Vijayakrishnan Prahlad

I

*Seven*. She discovers the mastiff's violence

on Dottie's fallen head—glass eyes sliding

into tilted sockets, her anguish simmering

when she weaves a lattice of fresh stitches,

looping them through the tubular neck

into the cotton mound of the doll's chest.

But the scaffolding fails and Dottie dangles,

decapitated again—dark curls, vinyl throat

florid from the ambush of teeth and claws—

irises frosted with the memory of mauling.

## II

*Twenty-seven.* She convulses and comes to
on the marble floor. Salt torches the fjords

in her lips as her left eye twitches and throbs,
an oozing plum—her pupils growing grey

with fear trapped in Dottie's tumbled resins.
She recalls a haze of whiskey, wildflowers,

flying arcs of frenzied fists, welts seared
on the pelt of her neck as starlings crowd

her windpipe—cold silhouettes of keyed dolls,
denied justice—marionettes in a godless night.

# The Saddest Place

Anon

We met in a café called *The Saddest Place*. We swapped stories – I was brave enough to say what happened to me as a twelve-year-old girl, not now brave enough to commit that man's act to a page. We talked for months, maybe more, all the women of this small country. We wondered what it would be like to run night-city streets, to walk in a dark forest unburdened. To do and wear what we liked without comment or shame. To stop the actions of those men who hold all the keys to the kingdom: the man who masturbated as myself and my sister made our way to the train, a too-handsy colleague at work too close beside me, the man whom I trusted as a girl, why me? Other women spoke of rape and violence. We held each other tight and cried then we spray-painted the walls of *The Saddest Place* with *Freedom, Fuck You, Take Back the Night*, yelling loud as we did so, yet still we all cried – the men jeering outside.

# Naqba

Beth Brooke

We are already deep into that night where
the unspeakable creeps out;

we sense the tapping of its spindle fingers
as it feels it way along the walls,

crawls to meet the rhythm of our hurrying feet;
we are anxious to reach the safety of home

where the lamps are lit and there are, we think,
no shadows to disquiet us.

We walk, try to keep ourselves from running,
but the monsters of our unfinished business

wait just ahead. Wraithlike, they slip in
behind us as we open the front door,

sit in our favourite chairs; their rictus smiles
greet us when we enter the sanctuary of our

living room and turn on the light.

# The One Time I Call 999 The Police Are Having A Party

Anna Shelton

how much have you had to drink how much have you had to drink how much have you had to drink how much have you had to drink how much alcohol did you drink how drunk are you how much have you had to drink laughter how much what time was this what time how much have you had to drink how long ago was this chink of glasses how much have you had to drink it's new year's eve how much have you had to drink deep laughter how much have you had to drink how many drinks how many hours ago was it how much have you had to drink please he's waiting how much have you had to drink how much have you had to drink how much have you had to drink how much have you had to drink how much have you drunk are you drunk how much have you had to drink how much have you had to drink have you been drinking how much have you had to drink I escaped how much have you had to drink how much have you had to drink how many drinks have you had please send someone how much have you had to drink sob how much have you had to drink how much have you had to drink how much have you had to drink how many drinks he's waiting for someone else how much have you had to drink how much have you had to drink how much have you had to drink how much have you had to drink party blowers toot how much have you had to drink listen love we're very busy here how much have you had to drink how much have you had to drink are you drunk how much have you had to drink men laughing how much have you had to drink how much have you had to drink dial tone

# Untitled

Sarah Connor

All the times I was ice

as if silence would be enough

and the times I was smoke,

slipping between the cracks in the world

and the times I was water, shaping

and reshaping myself.

I should have been fire.

I should always have been fire.

# Kemonomichi (Beast Trails)

Sharon SingingMoon

In defiance of prescribed paths
she surrendered
to yearnings for choice

chose resistance
rejected constructed identities
built of rigid expectations

found free-will ways
followed the illicit trails
created by secret wishes –

her own desire lines through
layers of man-made architecture
to where she is free.

# Street Talking
Alice Stainer

(*For women, confinement is always waiting to envelope you*).
*Rebecca Solnit*

Beyond your window, darkness crowds close
as a street-corner gang. The playmat of roads
is rolled away tight so it can't engross
your desire. Your game is not on foot. Modes
of retreat from the streets are underway:
trust that sturdy door, encompassing wall,
flagged bus if you must. At the end of the day
it's politic not to leave home at all.

But studded doors groan and grind on hinges:
the rooms are too full, too full of us all.
Walls clad in talk, we crouch in their angles
sharpen our pain with each one of us gone
till its edge glints true and we hack them all down
        spill out on the streets        spill out on the streets

# Biographies

**Beth Brooke** lives in Dorset and is a retired teacher. She is a twice nominated poet for the Pushcart prize and has three books of poems to her name, A Landscape With Birds and Transformations, both published by Hedgehog Press and Chalk Stories.

**Ronita Chattopadhyay** (she/her) finds refuge in words. Her poems have appeared in The Hooghly Review, Roi Fainéant Press, The Afterpast Review, Akéwì Magazine, Setu and Ghudsavar, among others. She lives in West Bengal, India, and works with not for profit organisations. Ronita loves books, mountains and tea.

**Roxane Llanque** is a Berlin writer and filmmaker. Her award-winning film "Aberration" was featured at numerous film festivals and her micro "The Tell-Tale Present" won 2023's Outstanding Miniature of World Pride Australia. Her poetry was published in Variety Pack and is forthcoming in the anthology "Thin Places & Sacred Spaces".

**Larissa Reid** is a poet and freelance science writer from Scotland's East coast. Notable publications include *Northwords Now, Black Bough Poetry, Reliquaie*, and various poetry anthologies including *Beyond the Swelkie* and *Mind the Links* (Tippermuir Books). She has three self-published pamphlets: *In February* (2019), *Caesura* (2022) and *rock|salt* (2022).

**Giovanna MacKenna** is currently poet in residence at the Wellcome Centre for Anti-Infectives Research, and part of the creative team working on Scotland's Covid Memorial project. Her first collection is available from The Museum of Loss and Renewal Publishing. For more info visit www.giovannamackenna.com and follow her on Instagram @giovmacpoet

**Christina Daub** has recent poems in *Bellevue Literary Review, Shō Poetry Journal, Gargoyle* and others. She also translates poetry from Spanish & German into English. She has taught poetry & creative writing at George Washington University among other schools. You can find her at christinadaub.com, christinadaub.bsky.social and @flix2fly on X

**Jane Killingbeck** is a new writer of poetry. She completed an MA in Creative Writing in 2023 exploring poetry for her final project under the tutelage of Mary Jean Chan. Her focus is familial relationships, love and belonging, real, remembered and imagined. Born in Yorkshire her sense of place features strongly in her poetry.

**Emma Galloway Stephens** is a creative writing educator who teaches in her hometown. She grew up in the Appalachian foothills of South Carolina. Her poems have appeared in *Catfish Stew, The Windhover, The Nature of Things,* and *Ekstasis Magazine.* She shares her life with her spouse and their strange pets.

**Lucy Heuschen** is a London-born poet living in Germany. Lucy's debut pamphlet was We Wear The Crown (Hedgehog, 2022). Her second pamphlet Loggerheads (Broken Spine) is due out in spring 2024. Her first collection will be published by Yaffle Press. Website:www.lucyheuschen.co.uk. X/Bluesky: PetiteCreature1

**Sarah-Jane Crowson's** art and poetry is inspired by ideas of accidental trespass, surrealism and romanticism. Her work can be seen in various places, including The Adroit Journal, Rattle, Petrichor, Sugar House Review and Iron Horse Literary Review. You can find her on Twitter @Sarahjf or at www.sarahjanecrowson.art.

**Allison Black** is a queer, neurodivergent, disabled writer who loves trees, birds and words. She has a BA in Creative and Professional Writing, and lives with a rescue cat named Astrid (who rescues her every day).

**Abigail Ottley** is an older woman writer and a former teacher from a strongly working class background. This year won the Wildfire Words flash fiction competition and was long listed for the Ink of Ages historical fiction prize. Born on the edge of London, she now lives in Cornwall.

**Jane Carroll** is an associate professor in children's literature. She writes fiction and creative non-fiction as well as academic work. She lives by the sea in north county Dublin with her husband, their daughter, and their eejit of a dog.

**Kerry Darbishire** lives in the English Lake District. Her poetry has won and been placed in many competitions. She is published widely in anthologies and magazines and has three poetry collections two pamphlets and a third to be published by Hedgehog Press in 2024.
Twitter contact: @kerrydarbishire

**Róisín Ní Neachtain** is a writer living in Kildare, Ireland. She has been published with Abridged, Firmament (Sublunary Editions), Broken Sleep Books and Poetry Jukebox. Her work was awarded the Dennis O'Driscoll Literary Bursary Award, second place at the Red Line and been shortlisted in a number of competitions.

**Nicola Heaney** is a poet from Derry, Northern Ireland. Her work has appeared or is upcoming in a number of journals across the UK and Ireland, including The North, Cormorant Broadsheet, Crannóg, Banshee and Poetry Birmingham Literary Journal. Her poetry has also been shortlisted for the Bridport Prize.

**Margaret Royall** has six poetry books to her name. She is widely published online and in print. Laurel prize nominated 2021 for 'Where Flora Sings'. Forthcoming in 2024 a new collection 'Toccata and Fugue' from Hedgehog Press and a chapbook 'Owl Fetish' from Dreich.
Website: Margaretroyall.com X @RoyallMargaret, Instagram @meggiepoet

**Ger Duffy's** poetry has been published by PNR, Southword, Poetry Ireland Review, Under the Radar, #Public Sector Poetry, The Ekphrastic Review, The Sailor Review, The Bangor Literary Journal, the Stony Thursday Book and other literary journals. She has been awarded mentoring awards by The MLC and the National Mentoring Board.

**Julia Biggs** is a poet, writer and freelance art historian. She lives in Cambridge, UK. Her work has appeared or is forthcoming in *Ink Sweat & Tears*, *Black Bough Poetry*, *Annie Journal*, *Sídhe Press*, *Streetcake Magazine* and elsewhere. Find her via her website: https://juliabiggs1.wixsite.com/juliabiggs

**Sue Finch's** first collection, 'Magnifying Glass', was published in 2020. Her work has also appeared in a number of online magazines. She loves the coast, peculiar things and the scent of ice-cream freezers. Find her via her website: https://suefinch.co.uk/

**Lynne Jensen Lampe's** poems appear in *Stone Circle Review*, *THRUSH*, *Yemassee*, and elsewhere. Her award-winning debut collection, *Talk Smack to a Hurricane* (Ice Floe Press, 2022) concerns mothers, daughters, mental illness, and antisemitism. She reads for *Tinderbox Poetry Journal* and lives in mid-Missouri with her husband and two dogs. https://lynnejensenlampe.com.

**Louise Machen** is a Mancunian poet with an MA in Creative Writing from The University of Manchester. Her work has most recently appeared in Cape Magazine and Acropolis Journal. She has nominations for the Pushcart Prize, Best of the Net and an upcoming collaborative pamphlet with Hedgehog Press (2024).

**Shasta Hanif Ali** is a writer and poet. Her writing delicately navigates the legacy of migration, race and heritage; where themes of memory and language interlace and disrupt. Shasta's writing has been published in the Scottish BPOC Writers Network, STV Scotland, The National and Our Time Is A Garden Anthology (IASH), among others.

**Annick Yerem** is a poet & the EIC of Sídhe Press. Her book, St.Eisenberg and the Sunshine Bus, was published with Hedgehog Press in 2022. You can find out more about her publications at annickyerem.eu or on Twitter & Bluesky @missyerem

**Mo Schoenfeld** has work in Irisi Magazine, Fevers of the Mind, Haiku Crush's Best Haiku Anthology 2021, 2022 & 2023 (Judges Grand Mention, 2022), Pure Haiku, Tiny Wren Lit, The Storms, Sídhe Press's 'Our Own Coordinates: Poems About Dementia' (guest editor) and their 'Glisk & Glimmer' anthology.
Bluesky: @moschoenfeld.bsky.social, Mastodon: @MoSchoenfeld@zirk.us

**Tamiko Dooley** read Latin and French at New College, Oxford. She was the winner of the BBC Radio 3 carol competition 2021. Her poem "Yurushi" was broadcast as BBC Radio 3's Friday poem in August 2023.

**Angela France** has had poems published in many of the leading journals and has been anthologised several times. Her fifth collection, *Terminarchy,* came out July 2021 (Nine Arches Press). Angela teaches creative writing at the University of Gloucestershire and in community settings. She runs a reading series in Cheltenham, 'Buzzwords'.

**Kitty Donnelly** has two collections of poetry published by Indigo Dreams. She won the Hammond House International Literary Prize in 2023. She has an MA in Creative Writing from Manchester Metropolitan University and a degree in Psychiatric Nursing. Her background is Irish and she currently lives in Yorkshire.

**Margaret Poynor-Clark** lives in East Lothian Scotland. She is interested in women's issues. She is also currently putting a pamphlet together about food. She has had poems published in Ink Sweat and Tears. She is a regular contributor to open mic sessions organised by the Rebecca swift Foundation.

**Moira J Saucer** is a disabled American poet holding an MFA from the University of Arkansas, Fayetteville. Her poems have appeared in journals and anthologies in the US, the UK, and Canada. Her debut chapbook, *Wiregrass and Other Poems* (November 2022), was published by Ethel.
Twitter: @MJSEyesOpened Bluesky: MJSEyesOpened

**Yvonne Reddick's** book *Burning Season* (Bloodaxe, 2023) received the Laurel Prize for Best First Collection of Ecopoetry and was shortlisted for the Saltire Scottish Poetry Book of the Year award. She worked with the filmmaker Aleksander Domanski to create the film *Searching for Snow Hares* (2023).

**Sarah Stockton** is the Editor-in-Chief of River Mouth Review. Her published poetry work includes: *Time's Apprentice* (dancing girl press, 2021) *Castaway* (Glass Lyre Press, 2022) and *The Scarecrow of My Former Self* (MoonPath Press, 2024).

**Sharon SingingMoon** is a poet & visual artist. She draws inspiration from Nature & our struggle to balance mind/body/spirit. Sharon has a Master's degree in Public Administration. Her poetry collections include *Random Seed* & *The Weight of One Hummingbird Feather,* both available at independent bookshops, Amazon & Barnes & Nobel

**Chaucer Cameron** is author of *In an Ideal World I'd Not Be Murdered* (Against The Grain 2021) She has been published in journals, and anthologies, including: *Poetry Wales,* and *Under the Radar*. She was shortlisted for *Live Canon International Poetry Competition 2021,* and co-edits the online magazine, *Poetry Film Live.*

**Attracta Fahy**, Psychotherapist, MA.W NUIG '17. Winner-Trócaire Poetry Ireland Competition 2021. Irish Times; New Irish Writing 2019, Placed 3rd, in Allingham Poetry Competition 2023. Shortlisted for: Saolta Poems for Patience 2023, Fish International Poetry Competition 2022. Fly Press published her debut chapbook collection Dinner in the Fields, in March'20.

**Jane Burn** is an award-winning hybrid writer. Her work is widely published. Her next collection, *The Apothecary of Flight*, will shortly be published by Nine Arches press. She is the Michael Marks Awards Environmental Poet of the Year 2023/24.

**Merril D. Smith** lives in southern New Jersey. Her poetry has been published in *Black Bough Poetry*, *Acropolis*, *Anti-Heroin Chic*, *The Storms*, *Fevers of the Mind*, *Humana Obscura, and Sidhe Press,* among other places. Her full-length collection, *River Ghosts (*Nightingale & Sparrow Press) was a Black Bough Press featured book.

British Iranian poet/ novelist **Afsaneh Gitiforouz** has performed at a host of poetry venues. She is a published poet including by Radical Roots, was commissioned to lead the poetry section of 'Age of Many Posts' at the Barbican in 2022 and is a committee member of the Exiled Writers Ink.

**Anna Shelton** is a teacher and writer from Cambridge. Her poem 'Black Fen' inspired her first folk song, which she performed at the 2022 Cambridge Folk Festival. She has been published in Coven and Streetcake magazine. She is currently writing her first pamphlet, which was longlisted for Verve in 2023.

**Oormila Vijayakrishnan Prahlad** is an Indian-Australian artist, poet, and improv pianist. Her chapbook, Patchwork Fugue, is forthcoming from Atomic Bohemian Press in February 2024. She lives and works in Sydney, on the traditional land of the Gammergal people.

**Sarah Connor`s** work can be found in multiple anthologies and magazines. Her books, The Crow Gods and The Poet Spells Her Name were published by Sídhe Press and by Black Bough Press. She has Pushcart and Best of Net nominations.

**Alice Stainer** teaches English Literature to visiting students in Oxford. Her work appears in *Atrium, Feral Poetry, Iamb, Dust, The Storms,* and *Ink, Sweat and Tears*, amongst other places, and has been nominated for prizes, including the Forward Prize. Her debut pamphlet is currently on submission.
Find her on X @AliceStainer

# Acknowledgements

*Childhood Ambition* by Beth Brooke, was previously published by Band of Bards, The Dark Side Of Purity.

*Untitled*, by Annick Yerem, is a black out/whiteout poem taken from the UN Statement, "The international community must "walk the talk" on the safety and security of women and girls in times of armed conflict: UN experts," International Day on the Elimination of Violence against Women, 24 November 2023.

https://www.ohchr.org/en/statements/2023/11/international-community-must-walk-talk-safety-and-security-women-and-girls-times

Printed in Great Britain
by Amazon